My First Book about the Alphabet of Coral Reef Animals
Volume I

Amazing Animal Books
Children's Picture Books

By Molly Davidson

Mendon Cottage Books

JD-Biz Publishing

Read **Volume II**

My First Book about the
Alphabet of Coral
Reef Animals
Volume II

Amazing Animal Books

Mendon Cottage Books

By Molly Davidson

Children's Picture Books

Purchase at Amazon.com

Download Free Books!

http://MendonCottageBooks.com

Introduction

Coral reefs are found on the coasts of most tropical oceans.

They only take up about 1% of the ocean floor, but about 25% of all marine fish live there.

 is for an Angelshark.

Angelsharks stay close to the bottom of the coral reefs in the sand during the day.

They hunt at night for fish, crustaceans, mollusks, and squid.

Their wide fins make them look like they have wings; this is why they are called angelsharks.

 is for a Blue Ring Octopus.

Elias Levy © <u>Wikimedia Commons</u>

The blue ring octopus, which is only about 8 inches long, is the World's most venomous octopus.

They can be found in the reefs surrounding Australia, New Guinea, Indonesia, and the Philippines.

C is for Coral.

Coral looks like a plant, but it is actually a living, breathing, and growing animal, which live in large groups, called colonies.

It starts out as a tiny polyp, when it lands on the ocean floor, it will never move from that location again.

D is for a Damselfish.

Damselfish are a species of brightly colored fish, which live in the anemones found in coral reefs.

About 1 out of every 4 eggs laid by the girl are eaten by the boy.

E is for an Emperor Red Snapper.

Emperor red snappers live in the shallow coral reef waters in the Indian and western Pacific Oceans.

The babies will hide safely under a sea urchin's spines until they are big enough to leave and eat on their own.

F is for Frogfishes.

Frogfishes are covered in spines or other sharp coverings which help to protect them.

They stay on the bottom of the coral reefs, trying to camouflage until they can strike, in a matter of milliseconds, their prey.

G is for Giant Clams.

Giant clams are the largest mollusks in the World, some growing to be over 6 feet long.

Many giant clams live to be over 100 years old.

They can release over 500 million eggs into the ocean at one time.

 **is for a Hermit Crab.**

Hermit crabs are not a true crab because as they grow they must find new shells to live in as protection.

They have 10 legs, the front two contain pinchers, and the back two are very short.

I

is for an Idolfish, specifically the Moorish Idol.

Moorish idol fish are found throughout the Indo-Pacific reefs, and are a very popular aquarium fish.

They eat mostly coral, sponges, and tunicates.

 **is for a Jellyfish.**

Jellyfish are made up of 98% water, and many are highly venomous, some strong enough to kill a human with one sting.

They can be any size from 2 cm to 3 feet in length.

K  is for a Krill.

Krill are a small shrimp that live in huge groups called swarms or clouds.

They stay at the bottom of the ocean during the day to avoid predators and swim to the surface at night to eat tiny organisms called phytoplankton.

L is for a Lobster.

Lobsters have a hard shell covering their body.

They are cold blooded; the temperature of the water controls their body temperature.

Lobsters never stop growing and can live to be over 100 years old.

 is for a Manatee.

Manatees, also called sea cows, eat the plants that grow in coral reefs.

They grow to be about 13 feet long and weigh about 1,300 pounds.

They spend about half their day sleeping.

 **is for a Necklace Starfish.**

Necklace Starfish grow to be about 12 inches across.

It likes to live in the rocky portions of the coral reef, eating sponges, algae, and small crustaceans.

O

is for an Opistognathidae, the scientific name for a Jawfish.

Michael Wolf © <u>Wikimedia Commons</u>

Jawfish live in burrows they dig on the bottom of the sandy ocean floor.

To protect their eggs, they keep them in their mouths until they hatch.

P is for a Pufferfish.

Pufferfish, also called blowfish, when in danger will suck up water which makes them puff out to be more than twice their normal size.

Inside their organs they have an extremely poisonous toxin called tetrodoxin.

Q is for a Queen Conch.

The queen conchs are a mollusk that lives inside large hard shells for protection.

The conch's mantle, a type of thin tissue, is what creates the hard, pink shell, which can grow to be over 1 foot in length.

 **is for a Ray.**

Rays are a flat fish that has no bones, only cartilage (the stuff your nose is made of).

They have spines on their tails which can sting their predators.

S is for a Sea Turtle.

Sea turtles are excellent swimmers and divers.

They cannot pull their head inside their shell like many land turtles can.

Every year the girls will swim thousands of miles to lay up to 200 eggs on the sandy beach where they were born.

T is for a Triggerfish.

There are over 40 different species of triggerfish; most live in the Indo-Pacific reefs.

The boys protect the eggs, and can get very aggressive if anything gets in their territory.

U is for an Urchin.

Sea urchins are a hard, spiny animal that moves very slowly along the bottom of the ocean floor.

They have venomous spines and their mouth is on the underside of their body.

 **is for a Vase Sponge.**

Vase sponges grow in most of the coral reefs around the World.

They are white or yellow and have a rough or hairy outer covering, sometimes they are smooth.

 **is for a White Tip Reef Shark.**

White tip reef sharks are a small shark, only growing to be about 5 feet long.

During the day, they stay inside underwater caves in the reefs, and then at night they come out and go hunting for fish, usually as a group.

 **is for Xenia Coral.**

Xenia is a soft coral, which has long arms and ends that look like flowers.

The flower heads can pulse, pushing water away from the group, or colony.

Y

is for a Yellow Longnose Butterflyfish.

This bright fish is most commonly found in the Indo-Pacific reefs and is popular in aquariums.

Butterflyfish are very protective, the girls protect the food, while the boys protect their territory.

 **is for Zooplankton.**

Matt Wilson/Jay Clark © <u>Wikimedia Commons</u>

Zooplanktons are tiny microscopic organisms that drift through the ocean water.

Many animals big, like whales, and small, snails, feed on zooplankton.

Conclusion

We hope you have enjoyed reading this book about all the amazing animals that live in coral reefs.

One more fact, the Great Barrier Reef around Australia is over 10,000 years old.

Our books are available at

1. Amazon.com

2. Barnes and Noble

3. Itunes

4. Kobo

5. Smashwords

6. Google Play Books

Download Free Books!
http://MendonCottageBooks.com

Publisher

JD-Biz Corp

P O Box 374

Mendon, Utah 84325

http://www.jd-biz.com/

.

www.ingramcontent.com/pod-product-compliance
Lightning Source LLC
Chambersburg PA
CBHW050856290526
45792CB00002B/622